RIDE TECHNOLOGY– REAP PROFITS

5 Secrets Every Footwear Distributor Must Know

RIDE
TECHNOLOGY–
REAP PROFITS

**5 Secrets Every Footwear Distributor
Must Know**

PARVEEN JAGGA

Worldwide Published by
Pendown Press

PENDOWN PRESS

An ISO 9001 & ISO 14001 Certified Co.,

Regd. Office: 2525/193, 1st Floor, Onkar Nagar-A,

Tri Nagar, Delhi-110035

Ph.: 09350849407, 09312235086

E-mail: info@pendownpress.com

Branch Office: 1A/2A, 20, Hari Sadan, Ansari Road,

Daryaganj, New Delhi-110002

Ph.: 011-45794768

Website: PendownPress.com

First Edition: 2023

ISBN: 978-93-5554-504-6

Layout and Cover Designed by Pendown Graphics Team

Printed and Bound in India by Thomson Press India Ltd.

*For my Parents, Who gave me
Everything And always seem to find
a way to give more.*

Contents

I CAN, I WILL!

My humble gratitude to my GURU Shyam Taneja & the I Lead Community.

This book is dedicated to
my distributors-
my HUMSAFARS,
the backone of the business.

Together we are strong
and prosperous...

Acknowledgements

I want to express my heartfelt gratitude to the many people who supported me in my life journey and the birth and completion of this book.

This book is the culmination of nearly 2 decades of learning and experience and wouldn't have been possible without the significant guidance, blessings, support and encouragement of a multitude of people. I thank each of you for walking with me on my life path.

To begin with, I wish to thank my parents, who gave me birth and the values that make me a worthy human being. It is their upbringing that makes it possible for me to live my purpose, of which this book is a part.

Next, I want to thank my Guru, Shyam sir, who triggered a paradigm shift in my being and helped me tap into my true potential.

A very special thanks to my loving wife Shreshtha and daughter Nysha for the joy they bring to my life.

Immense gratitude to my brothers Vishal and Nishant, as well as the rest of my family and friends, for their love, care, patience and unspoken support.

Huge thanks to my mentor Akshar Yadav, who inspired me to write this book and helped me grow.

I also acknowledge Rajan Guha & Khushwant Sharma, who add much value to my life and always help and support me in every aspect.

I am thankful to My Friend Dinesh Verma, CEO, Pendown Press and his team for their support and suggestions throughout the creative process.

Finally, much gratitude to Team Alfa for their unconditional support and care.

"*Every life has a story.*
Every story has a lesson."
~Anonymous

My Story: Straight From My Heart To Yours

Hello, my name is Praveen Jagga. I am a Footwear Manufacturer and a Footwear Technology Expert.

This book is a gift as a part of my service journey to all my Channel Partners & Dealers, who I lovingly call my "HUMSAFARS" (meaning those who journey with us on our life path).

Let me start my story right from the beginning and how it all culminated in writing this book.

I was born into a family that was already deep into footwear manufacturing, so it would not be wrong to say that this business runs in my blood and is my destiny.

My father owned a footwear manufacturing business that was spread successfully across the entire state of Haryana under the brand name "Today Footwear".

Not being keen on academics, I decided to join the family business immediately after graduation. Though not inclined toward studies, I had the intuitive wisdom to know that in order to truly excel at something, one should have knowledge of that subject or industry. Toward this end, I completed a Diploma in Footwear Design from the well-known Footwear Designing & Development Institute, Noida, before joining the family business.

Finally, with big dreams in my eyes, I entered the family business alongside my father and was determined to work hard to scale up the business and make my father immensely proud of me.

However, I soon realized that there existed a gap between theoretical and practical knowledge and to bridge this gap, I spent hours and hours on the Shop Floor trying to learn as much as I could from the experienced and skilled workforce.

Obviously, no learning graph is a smooth line, and neither was mine. In the process of learning, I made many mistakes, but I made sure to learn the lesson and move forward.

It was my dream to take our brand pan India instead of being captive to Haryana only. I worked ceaselessly toward this goal, and soon ultimately, we had an impactful pan-India presence.

The business grew, my father's joy and reputation grew, and our profits grew. I had it all the money, the huge factory, the big houses, the fancy cars, the exotic foreign vacations, and a loving family, and despite my busy schedule, I made it a point to enjoy life and always maintain a work-life balance.

However, there was something else that grew alongside the business, profits and joy. It was a strange restlessness and discontent that I could not put my finger upon.

All Is Not Well

> *"You were put on this earth to achieve your greatest self, to live out your purpose, and to do it courageously."*
> ~Steve Maraboli

Up until now, though I had worked pretty hard, my life had been more or less smooth. Here, however, was the start of a different chapter. I felt bored, restless and discontented despite having everything. All the dreams and goals that I had begun my journey with were fulfilled. The spark in my life was totally missing. I was besieged by a deep sense of emptiness. It was definitely time to dream bigger and aim higher.

I had this feeling deep down that I was meant to do something bigger, that there had to be more to life than the routine of business or pleasure. Surely there must be more meaning to life. People around me felt I was mad, and some thought I was greedy. Everyone kept saying that you have enough to last lavishly for a lifetime and for the next generations to live luxuriously, what more do you want? Yet I knew there had to be another purpose to my life.

As the wise say, when the student is ready, the master appears, and I, too, was fortunate to find a Guru who taught me that when your personal goals stop exciting you: it is time to think bigger, it is time to serve society and humanity at large.

Since it is a technology-driven world today, so my inner voice kept telling me that my purpose should be about using technology for the benefit and growth of the footwear industry. However, I knew nothing about technology except its spelling. I was completely clueless about where to begin.

The Universe Has Your Back

> *"When you're connected to the power of intention, everywhere you go and everyone you meet is affected by you and the energy you radiate. As you become the power of intention, you'll see your dreams being fulfilled almost magically, and you'll see yourself creating huge ripples in the energy fields of others by your presence and nothing more."*
>
> **~Wayne W. Dyer**

However, when your intention is selfless and to serve, the Universe fills you up with renewed energy and guides you intuitively.

I found this challenge exciting and fastened my seat belt to take it head-on and succeed. I made a vision plan to become the means to provide employment to at least 10,000 people by the year 2025 in the footwear industry through creating and building a technology-driven Company.

A Leap of Faith

> *"An arrow can only be shot by pulling it backwards. So when life is dragging you back with difficulties, it means that it's going to launch you into something great. So just focus, and keep aiming."*
> **~ Paulo Coelho**

Now we are all aware that to take a huge leap, we must take a few steps back and gain momentum for the leap. My case was no different; in trying to do something new and challenging, I faced many setbacks. People felt my dreams were unrealistic and impossible. They were unwilling to support me, and many even disassociated themselves from me.

Almost everyone close to me has doubts about the path I was taking and were worried that I would fail.

That was the darkest nightmare possible. I didn't know what to do and where to begin. It hurt me no end.

But it was the unsaid best wishes and love of those same near and dear ones that protected me and made me strong enough to overcome all the challenges.

Though it was quite painful, I understood deep down that asking me not to move forward with my ambitious plans was their way of trying to protect me from failure.

I hope and pray that after reading this book, not only will my own family be proud of me and other parents will also be motivated to encourage and support their children in pursuing their dreams even if they are not so sure of them.

I, however, knew this was my life purpose, my calling and I knew I was meant to be a problem solver and a solution provider. I was determined to change the face of the footwear industry through the magic of technology. I was determined to be a modern-day Alibaba of this industry.

But in the face of constant and strong criticism from friends and peers, even I began to buckle down. Regrettably, I began to doubt myself and my dreams and was almost ready to give up on them, but the Universe, of course, had other plans.

To motivate myself, I read Elon Musk's biography, and it inspired me no end. I thought if he could have the courage and determination to build an entire world on another planet, I could certainly dream of doing something new here without being disheartened.

So, I began working toward my vision. Since I was clueless about technology, I dived wholeheartedly into learning about it. I read books, attended courses, talked to experts and gathered knowledge from every source possible.

Despite having been at the top of my game, I became a humble student again, even to the extent of working in a technology-driven company as an employee. Being the owner of a fair-sized business, it was not an easy task but fulfilling my purpose was all I could focus on. I was like Arjun, seeing nothing but my goal.

I was convinced that if I had to do something big, it would be possible only through technology. After 3 years of sincere dedication, single-minded focus and immense hard work, I mastered technology and set up a technology Company providing solutions to the footwear industry.

There is a Solution to Every Problem

> *"Every problem has a solution; it may sometimes just need another perspective."*
> **~Katherine Russell**

Having understood that I was here on this planet earth by the grace of the Almighty to be a Problem Solver and Solution Provider, I researched deeply to discover where I could contribute. Here my vast experience in the footwear industry came into play, and I realized that there were many challenges that my Humsafars-my channel partners were facing (some that they were even unaware of, so obviously, how could they address them) which could be overcome with the help of technology.

Leveraging technology would not only help our channel partners in identifying the market potential, penetrating new markets, forecasting trends, optimizing inventory and facilities, managing the supply chain, optimizing delivery and reducing returns, but it would also benefit our customers greatly.

When implemented, these technology-driven solutions work like magic to enhance productivity, sales & marketing and ultimately, profitability.

Technology is the doorway to prosperity—further in this book, I will share each of these technology-driven magical solutions with you in detail.

So that is the story of how I found my calling and my life purpose and how this book reached your hands.

Without further ado, lets deep dive into the real magic of technology driven profitability.

Khul ja sim sim…

"If we're not doing better, it's almost always our own inability to execute, not because someone else is stealing our market share or something."

~Evan Sharp

Secret #2

Mining The Market
To The Maximum

So before we address how you can leverage technology to overcome your challenges and become profitable in the footwear industry, let's address the most important concern that never fails to come up.

A concern that I often hear from my dealers and distributors- my Humsafars is that, *"Market mandaa hai."* (मार्किट मंदा है) meaning the market is slow. That how do we do more business, there is not enough potential.

My message to you is simple: Yes I know you are doing your best and working hard.

BUT, are You WORKING SMART????

Have you really given it all you've got?

Have you ever tried to dig a little deeper to find out what is the potential of the market in your area of operation?

Let me tell you something, you will be not just surprised but shocked to know that despite all your effort, you are merely skimming the surface of the market.

If you work smart using technology driven solutions to research, and enhance all deliverables you will see that it is not the market that is slow or limited. It is your way of working that is keeping you and your market share limited.

Now, I am sure, your next question will be, well how do I know what exactly is the potential of the market in my particular area?

Okay so this is a very simple but powerful eye-opening exercise that I am sharing with you right here & now.

- Sit down with a pen, paper and calculator in front of your laptop.

- First off let me tell you as per market research 1 person buys an average of 1.7 pairs of footwear in a year.

- Now open your laptop and google the population in your area of dealership/distributorship.

- Multiply this population by 1.7 and there you have the number of pairs of footwear that the population in your area needs and is likely to buy.

- That, my dear friends is your market potential right in front of you for the entire year.

- That is business not just on paper but literally being offered to you on a platter.

- Now check your computer for the business you have done and you will know what share of the market you have penetrated and what more is yours for the taking, if you do things right.

The Indian footwear industry valued at US$ 13.49 Billion in 2021 is expected to grow at a CAGR of 12.83% through 2022 to 2027, reaching nearly US$ 27.84 Billion.4.39.

So the fault and limitations as you can see lie not with the market but with our very own way of working.

As a footwear and technology expert, I can guarantee you that with the right technology solutions that I will be sharing with you in detail in the chapters to come, nothing can stop you from mining the market potential to the maximum and becoming a profitable market leader.

I have worked extensively in my own business and then researched the challenges and problems of the dealers and distributors in the footwear industry first hand by meeting nearly 500 of them personally.

I can safely guarantee you that I understand each and every operational and marketing challenge and can undoubtedly say that TECHNOLOGY is the solution to each and every challenge.

So let us dive into the world of technology and learn how to leverage it to grow your business and profitability.

Success Exercise #1

Break Limitations: Claim Your Market Share

[Material needed: A pen, paper, calculator, access to internet & your business details either on desktop/laptop/ mobile phone.]

The Population in your area of operation:

____

____

____

____

Remember Golden Rule: 1 person buys an average of 1.7 pairs of footwear in a year.

Your Market Potential = Population in your area X 1.7

____

____

____

____

Your Actual Business Turnover:

____

____

____

____

The Business you are missing out on=
Population in your area X 1.7 - Your Actual Business Turnover

____

____

____

____

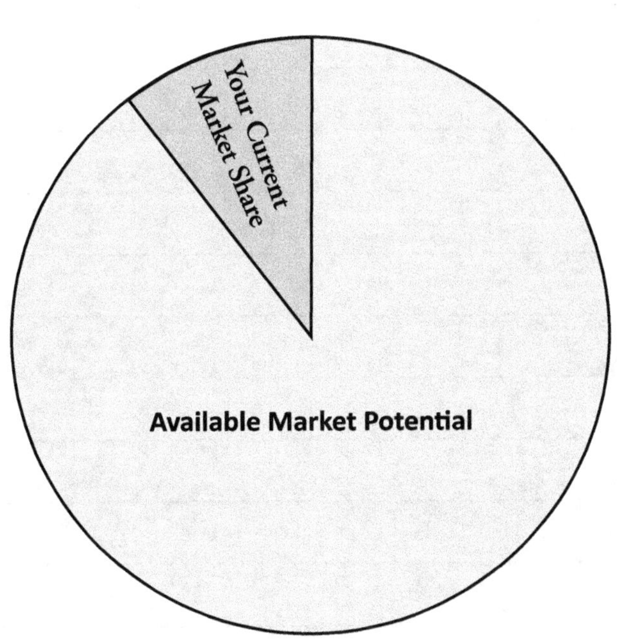

Notes:

"Every problem has a solution". I have never come across a problem which couldn't be solved. However, in order to solve a problem, we need two things—

(a) Define what the problem is?

(b) Take ownership to find a solution to your problem and stay committed until you find a solution."

~Sanjeev Himachali

Challenging
The Challenges And Winning

As we have discussed in the previous chapter, the footwear industry is an ascending industry with ample scope for growth, yet most of us in the business are unable to exploit its full potential. This is because we are unable to overcome the bottlenecks and challenges that this industry is fraught with.

The challenges that this industry faces are many; however, thankfully, the solution is one-stop-TECHNOLOGY.

Challenges in the Footwear Industry

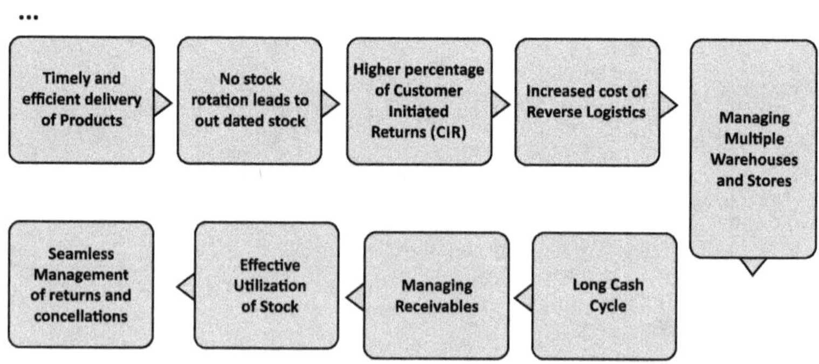

These challenges will fall under three major heads.

Order Management & Fulfillment- Return Management

The challenges faced in this area are:

- Timely and efficient delivery of products.
- Poor order management leading to cancelled orders.
- Higher percentage of customer returns.
- Low management of returns & nonexistent return management system.
- Simplified order & fulfillment system
- Inefficient utilization of stocks.

Inventory Management

The challenges faced in this area are:

- No Stock rotation leading to outdated Stocks.
- Managing multiple warehouses and stores.
- Lack of a proper inventory management system.
- No warehouse management system.
- No stock aging report.

Cash Flow and Credit Management

The challenges faced in this area are:

- Cash flow management.
- No track of receivables.
- No bad debt recovery mechanism.
- No debtor and creditors track reports.

- No progress report tracking.

All these challenges are causing you to leak profits, and the worst part, my friends, is that you are not even aware of these losses.

And all this is happening because you are continuing to stick to your age-old traditional methods instead of letting technology enable you to integrate all your operations and manage everything smoothly and profitably.

Using technology-enabled integrated software systems, each challenge can be managed. Now you may be wondering how that would be possible.

Technology is the present and the future. It plays a huge role in the modern era, and only those who learn to integrate and leverage it in their lives and businesses will thrive. Technology is the need of humanity and business today.

Traditional methods and systems will keep you limited. It is only through Technology that we can scale up and grow exponentially.

Today data and information are the pillars of the economy as they are essential to making informed decisions. Analyzing data is critical to making profitable decisions and tweaking systems and processes. All successful businesses today are based on data-driven decision-making.

In the following chapters, I will discuss each challenge and its technology solution in detail.

So, let's get set and gooooo...

"What you cannot see, you cannot address and resolve. Order Kills due to mismanagement are silent Killers."

~Praveen Jagga, Technology Expert

Secret #4

Stop Leaking Profits!
Manage Orders & Returns
With Technology

Leaking Profits

Friends & Humsafars, let's look at how we all regularly manage our orders traditionally.

Whether you are a distributor or retailer, once you receive an order, in all likelihood, it is either noted down in your diary or, at best, entered into an excel sheet.

As a distributor, suppose you deal with around 250 retailers; imagine the multiple orders you must receive from each distributor.

For a hypothetical example, let's say each retailer places an average of 20 orders simultaneously. The math is quite simple- you will likely be handling at least 5000 orders at any given time.

That is huge!

Now, imagine handling and following up on all these orders from a diary or even an excel sheet, for that matter. It is indeed a mind-boggling task.

Once you place the order with the respective companies, you will surely forget to follow up on at least some of them. In fact, I have even witnessed instances where the order came in from the retailer and was noted down in the diary but unfortunately was not in stock and never got placed with the right company as there were too many orders to manage.

It stayed noted and hidden in the corner of the diary- never seeing the light of the day!

Think of all the times you check your diary and follow up on the orders; you do it a maximum of 3-4 times and then move on to the more recent orders.

And what happens to those orders, my friend? Well, it's a game of chance- some come through, and that's great. Regrettably, many get lost in the chaos of the pages of the diary, and the order gets killed instead of being fulfilled!

And the worst part is that you do not even notice or realize how many orders are silently killed.

And obviously, you cannot correct what you do not see!

This silent killing of orders continues, and you keep leaking profits as each unfulfilled order is a direct loss, even though it may not be directly visible.

Let me explain this better with some hypothetical figures,

Supposing your total turnover is 5 Cr rupees and your profit margin is 10%.

This means your profit is 50 Lakh rupees.

But imagine that you are also losing and not fulfilling 10 % of your orders due to your invisible mismanagement of orders.

Then you are also losing orders close to 50 Lakh Rupees.

Continuing with the assumption of a profit margin of 10 %, this means you are losing 5 Lakh rupees straight away without even knowing it.

Using the Gift of Technology Profitably

On the other hand, if you were to use Technology for order management, tracking and fulfillment, you would never again lose a single penny of profits.

By adopting a world-class advanced and integrated, yet simple and easy-to-use technology system developed for footwear distributors and retailers specifically, you would:

- Be able to supply the order immediately and efficiently if in stock, as with the click of a finger, your screen will show you whether you have the required inventory or not. [No wastage of time, and other resources, no duplication of order placement and burden of extra inventory].

- Also, immediate action means efficient and timely delivery of products which not only boosts your reputation, and builds customer delight and loyalty but also means a shorter cash cycle leading to liquid assets.

- If the required material is not in stock with you, using the Vendor Management Program of your Technology enabled system, you will be able to place the order on the right vendor with the fastest TAT (Turn-Around-Time immediately.

- With the Order Management & Tracking System, you will be able to follow up and track your order in real-time right until you receive it. This way, if there is any delay in order processing, your system will automatically raise the alarm, and you will be able to manage or resolve the bottleneck at the earliest. In such a scenario, you can keep the customer in the loop, too; this way, they won't be annoyed, and you will not lose them.

- Thirdly with the Simplified Order Fulfillment System, you will be able to keep track of what percentage of orders you have fulfilled, and then you can further analyze and rectify the reasons for the unfulfilled ones.

Manage Your Orders and their Fulfillment easily with live tracking, updates and reminders.

Using Technology, you can manage, place and track your order even on your mobile phone at the single click of a finger.

And I guarantee you that with a technology-enabled system in place will, YOU WILL STOP LEAKING PROFITS SILENTLY!

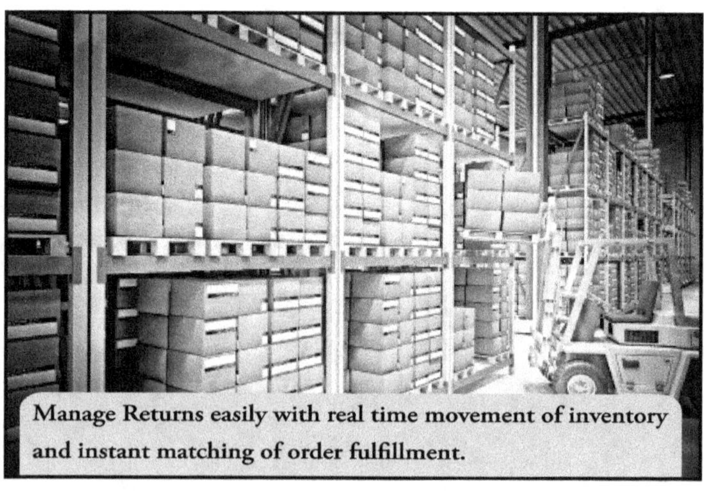

Manage Returns easily with real time movement of inventory and instant matching of order fulfillment.

Managing Returns Profitably with Technology

Returns are part and parcel of business, and bringing them down to zero is impossible. However, returns don't need to be the cause of leaking profits.

In the traditional system, when a return comes in, it is simply acknowledged and put into the warehouse and then usually forgotten about until the end of the financial year or when taking physical inventory.

And then they will be on sale at heavy discounts, even up to 70%. This spells a significant loss to your business.

However, with a Technology driven integrated system in place, you wouldn't have to bear these losses.

When a return came in, it would immediately be recorded in the system, and you could view it with a click when checking the inventory. If it fits the requirement of a new order, it could be immediately utilized, and the order could be dispatched quickly.

This would not only ensure timely delivery but also would mean optimum utilization of stock. There would not be any duplicity of orders and inventory, and also, there would be no need to sell the dead returns at deeply discounted prices inducing losses and leaking profits.

Also, through this system, you could calculate the Return Ratio easily and then analyze and rectify the reasons behind those returns to ensure higher profitability.

Thus Technology is the path to profitability. Embrace it NOW & STOP LEAKING PROFITS!

Success Exercise # 2

Stop Leaking Profits : Map Your Invisible Losses

The losses incurred due to not fulfilling orders and managing returns are huge but invisible as they don't show up on your balance sheet. These invisible losses can be stopped by adopting technology driven solutions.

When you perform the exercises given below, you will be shocked to see the results and will realize how you have been bleeding your hard-earned money without knowing it.

[You will need: A pen, paper, calculator and access to your business details]

1.

    a. Track and calculate the value of orders received in the last 6 months: _______________________

    ____

    b. Track and calculate the value of orders you actually fulfilled in the last 6 months:_______________________

    ____

Your Invisible Loss = 1-2

2.

    a. Track & calculate the value of your total returns in the last 6 months:_______________________

    ____

b. Track and calculate the value of returns matched to orders at full price _______________________________

____

c. Track and calculate the value of returns sold at discounted prices _______________________________

____

Your Invisible Loss = 1-2-3

Notes:

"The more inventory a company has, the less likely they will have what they need."

~Taiichi Ohno

Dead Stocks = Dead Business Manage Inventory Profitably With Technology

The Chaos of Physical Inventory

If I were to ask you whether you are even aware of what you have in stock or what is the best-selling item in your inventory, tell me honestly would you have an answer?

Also, are you even aware of how much unnecessary duplicate inventory you have? Do you know that the last lot of footwear you ordered consisted of items that had not been moving during the previous six months because the fashion trends have changed?

In addition, because you do not know what is in stock when new orders come in, you, in turn, get new material to fulfill those orders because there is no accurate real-time technology to tell you that you already have these pieces in stock. And, of course, checking inventory physically on a daily basis to match order fulfillment is not possible.

In the chaos of your regular manual/physical inventory system (an Excel sheet or Tally at best), it is unlikely that you will find what you need when you need it. In such a scenario, your inventory, instead of serving you as an asset, becomes a liability to your business as an added cost.

The Gift of Technology

On the other hand, if you opt for a Technology-driven inventory management system,

- The first benefit would be that you would have a bird's eye view of your entire inventory in real-time at just the click of your mouse or your phone. This means that you can match inventory to orders immediately and speedily to avoid duplicity of stock altogether.

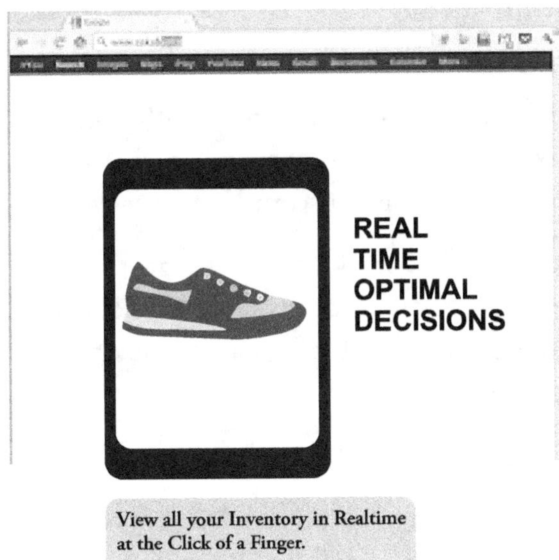

View all your Inventory in Realtime at the Click of a Finger.

- Secondly, a stock turnover ratio report would give you a clear picture of which of your stock items are moving and at what pace. Knowing this would help you decide what to order and what not accordingly. Without knowing for sure what moves, you are like a blind man ordering either according to your own choice/gut or as per the company representative's recommendation.

And neither of these is the right way of forecasting inventory because your choice is not necessarily everybody's choice. The company representative could also have vested interests and push products with more margin for them or their own dead stock.

I have personally witnessed distributors ordering all colors and sizes of a product just to ensure they are well stocked (without knowing what has moved for them in the past).

And where does this lead you? With your liquid assets blocked as dead inventory, that will perhaps never sell or, at best, sell at a massive discount.

However, with a stock turnover ratio to guide you, you would never go wrong. You would base your ordering and stocking on actual proof of what is moving and not on random parameters.

Find & Focus On Your Bestsellers through Stock Turnover Ratio

- Thirdly, with advanced Technology, you would have a stock aging report in your hands so that you could work out ways and means to promote the stuck stock on time while it's still of value.

An advanced Technology-driven warehouse management system would also make life simple and profitable for you by giving you FIFO reports and alerts. With such a system, you could implement FIFO-based stock picking and cycle count to greatly impact stock management and profitability.

Inventory is the core of your entire business; if the core is mismanaged, the whole business will be affected badly.

Managing your inventory well means a direct saving in your working capital, and a saving in cost always leads to more profits.

Success Exercise # 3

1. Track and calculate the value of duplicate orders you placed on companies due to mismanagement of inventory in the last 6 Manage Your Inventory : Curtail Your Losses

2. [You will need: A pen, paper, calculator and access to your business details]

3. Months ____

    ____

4. Track and calculate the value of inventory sold at discounted prices due to aging in the last 6 months

    ____

5. Track and calculate the value of the dead inventory that has not moved in the last 6 months

    ____

Your Invisible Loss = 1+2+3

Notes:

"Never take your eyes off the cash flow because it's the lifeblood of business."
~Sir Richard Branson

Cash Flow Is King!
Manage Debtors & Creditors Profitably With Technology

Cash flow and credit management are critical areas of any business.

In the traditional way of doing business, generally, just as there is no tracking of orders, there is no regular tracking of receivables. Who owes you what is looked at only once in a while by the accountant, either as an infrequent ritual or in times of a cash crunch?

Leave alone following up; there are times when even the invoice is not raised on time.

From all this, it follows that there is no bad debt recovery mechanism and no identification of defaulters in payment, and we keep supplying them despite these being unprofitable transactions.

Technology Manages Cash Flow & Creditors

With Technology, it's possible to turn this situation around with great ease.

Because you do not have a debtors and creditors track report, you do not know who is paying you up front, within the stipulated credit period or paying you late.

Without this knowledge, you keep servicing them equally. In contrast, if you focused on and maximized transactions with those who pay upfront or on time and stopped or at least minimized supplies to those paying late, your cash flow cycle would be shorter and financial health would always be great.

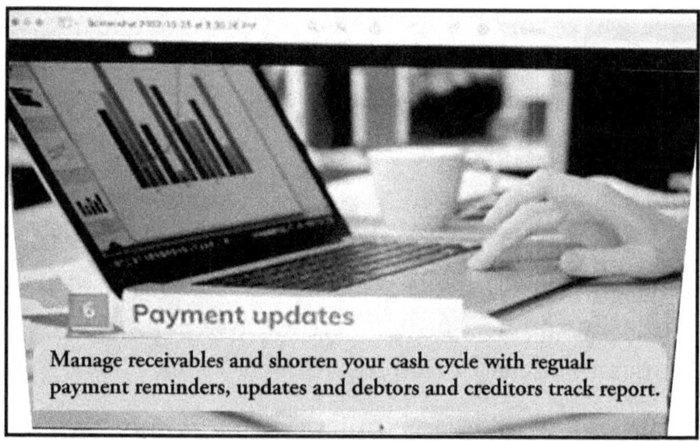

Manage receivables and shorten your cash cycle with regualr payment reminders, updates and debtors and creditors track report.

These people who make late payments or don't pay impact your business hugely.

Since your payments don't come on time, you cannot pay your suppliers on time and have to take loans from the bank, market or friends and family to meet your financial commitments. You not only end up paying interest on those loans, but you also undergo a lot of distress, and your reputation, too, takes a hit.

Have you ever stopped to think how this interest on the loan that you pay is a significant loss and eats into your profits?

If you ever sat down to calculate it, you would be shocked!

It is an unfortunate loss that can be easily stopped by shifting operations to a Technology-driven creditor-debtor management system.

With this system in place, you can also be assured that your bill or invoice will be raised on time.

And it will also ensure that it alerts you to have a fool-proof payment follow-up mechanism.

Success Exercise # 4

Manage Your Receivables: Increase Your Cash Flow.

[You will need: A pen, paper, calculator and access to your business details]

1. Track all payments that have been received after the due date or have not been received at all in the last 6 months. And then calculate the amount of interest you could have earned on that money for the period of time that money would have been with you______

   ____

2. Calculate the value of any interest you had to pay on loans taken (if taken) to fulfill your financial obligations due to not receiving your payment on time________

   ____

3. Calculate the value of any penalties you had to pay for not meeting your financial commitments due to not receiving your payments on time ____________

   ____

Your Invisible Loss = 1+2+3

Notes:

The Path To Profitability
An Overview To Conclude

As I said earlier, I am on a mission to impact 10,000 families.

My primary goal is to make business smoother and more profitable for my Humsafars- my distributors and dealers in every way that I can.

Toward this end, I have developed an integrated technology solution to overcome all their challenges with ease and enhance profits exponentially.

Due to these constant efforts toward helping my distributors and dealers leverage the power of technology to drive profitability, I have been privileged to be nominated for the Startup Awards in the Technology & Innovation section by the Entrepreneur magazine at the Startup Summit 2023.

Also, this book you are holding in your hands right now was launched at the prestigious Author's corner at the New Delhi World Book Fair, Pragati Maidan, 2023, which is one of the highest honor for a book.

Addressing the press, audience and government policymakers during the Q & A at the launch, I was privileged to have an awesome response to the valuable, eye-opening insights offered by this book.

In addition to all this, as a manufacturing partner, I have gone and progressively disrupted the market with an irresistible offer for my Humsafars.

This incredible offer will make life easy and profitable for you.

When you order a footwear product of your choice in the market, by default, you get a packaging of 36 pairs of shoes, whether you need it or not. And you are stuck with unnecessary inventory that blocks your cash flow.

So we offer you a choice of packaging for 12 pairs of shoes.

Hassle-free doorstep delivery.

And an easy seven-day return policy.

Now you have 2 choices:

Either

You can carry on in the traditional manner that you have been doing and continue leaking profits without knowing it.

Or

You can shift to a technology-driven integrated solution designed specifically for all your challenges as a footwear distributor that will help you be exponentially profitable by cutting down your cost of operations, shortening your cash cycle, delivering on time and managing your inventory.

This will also allow you to be stress-free with more time on your hands to focus on scaling up your business.

If you choose to focus on profitability and step onto the path of technology, reach out to us.

As an entrepreneur, it is my Dharma to be of service and guide other entrepreneurs on the path of tech-driven profitability. It is my heartfelt desire that my Humsafar should be the topmost distributor/dealer in their area.

If you want sure shot results in your business in the fastest timeframe, book a discovery call to diagnose your business and seal the profit leakages forever.

I will help you achieve 10X growth and become the top distributor/dealer in your city.

Book your Discovery Call here.

Notes:

Notes:

Notes: